IT'S A WONDERFUL LIFE

A Play in Two Acts

From the film
by
FRANK CAPRA
and the story
by
PHILIP VAN DOREN STERN

Adapted for the stage
by
JAMES W. RODGERS

Dramatic Publishing
Woodstock, Illinois • London, England • Melbourne, Australia

IT'S A WONDERFUL LIFE

A Play In Two Acts
For 12 Men, 10 Women, 2-4 young boys and 2 young girls

CHARACTERS
(In order of appearance)

GEORGE BAILEY . . . . the Everyman of Bedford Falls
CLARENCE ODBODY . . . . A-S-2 (Angel Second Class)
MR. GOWER . . . . proprietor of the corner drug store
YOUNG GEORGE . . . . .age 12
HARRY BAILEY . . . . George's younger brother
MOTHER BAILEY . . . a very kind and understanding woman
AUNT TILLY . . . . Uncle Billy's wife
VIOLET PETERSON . . . . proprietor of a beauty salon
BERT . . . . a patrolman
ERNIE . . . . a mail carrier
UNCLE BILLY . . . . .George's uncle and business partner
MARY HATCH (later Mary Bailey) . . . George's loving wife
HENRY F. POTTER . . . . owns practically the entire town
MR. POTTER'S GOON . . . . ever-present with Mr. Potter
MR. POTTER'S SECRETARY . . . ever-faithful to Mr. Potter
MRS. HATCH . . . . Mary's mother
SAM WAINWRIGHT . . . a financially successful young man
MISS ANDREWS . . . . a townsperson
MRS. THOMPSON . . . . a townsperson
MR. MARTINI . . . . proprietor of a bar
MRS. MARTINI . . . . his wife
MISS CARTER . . . . .a bank examiner
NEWSPAPER BOY . . . . .age 10
PETE BAILEY . . . . .age 12

TOMMY BAILEY ....age 10
ZUZU BAILEY ....age 7
MR. WELCH .... the schoolteacher's husband
JANIE BAILEY ....age 9

Doubling possible for: Young George and Pete Bailey
                          Tommy Bailey and Newsboy

Other doubling possible, if necessary.

  Note: It is strongly recommended that your production be
staged on a unit set with minimal set pieces and carefully
planned costume changes. It is most important that the actors
be able to move from scene to scene without blackouts or
pauses of any kind.

SETTING: Christmas Eve, Bedford Falls. 1945

TIME: Early evening.

IT'S A WONDERFUL LIFE was first presented at Paul Laurence Dunbar High School in Lexington, Kentucky, on December 15, 1993. It was produced and directed by Trish Clark with Set Design by Karl Anderson, Lighting Design by Jeff Fightmaster, and Costume Design by Marie Henderson. The cast, in order of appearance, was as follows:

George Bailey	*Bob Martin*
Clarence Odbody	*John Tackett*
Mr. Gower	*Spencer Christensen*
Young George	*Thad Watson*
Harry Bailey	*Carter Adler*
Mother Bailey	*Kelly McHone*
Aunt Tilly	*Stephanie Mills*
Violet Peterson	*Berry Seelbach*
Bert	*George Spellman*
Ernie	*Kris Singeton*
Uncle Billy	*Sean Zehnder*
Mary Hatch	*Kelli Stinnett*
Henry F. Potter	*Langston Hemenway*
Mr. Potter's Goon	*Shawn Jacob*
Mr. Potter's Secretary	*Stacey Carpenter*
Mrs. Hatch	*Sara Feagan*
Sam Wainwright	*Daniel Melcher*
Miss Andrews	*Sara Fegan*
Mrs. Thompson	*Taylor Baker*
Mr. Martini	*Tony Manuel*
Mrs. Martini	*Sybil Dawahare*
Miss Carter	*Garrett Graddy*
Newspaper Boy	*Thad Watson*
Pete Bailey	*Thad Watson*
Tommy Bailey	*Brad Metzger*
Zuzu Bailey	*Ashley Metzger*
Mr. Welch	*Joe Mike Anderson*
Janie Bailey	*Krista Metzger*

WHAT PEOPLE ARE SAYING about *It's a Wonderful Life...*

"I am impressed with the faithful adaptation of this classic story. Audiences enter, expecting the story they know and love, and that's exactly what they get!"

Ken Barnett, Mount Gilead High School, Mount Gilead, Ohio

"An excellent adaptation of the classic film. Very theatrical. All the most-loved scenes from the film are included."

Don Swarz, Starry Night Theatre, Inc., North Tonawanda, N.Y.

"This is an excellent play for high school production. It is difficult to find crowd-pleasing plays for this size group and this one had a good variety of smaller parts along with automatic crowd appeal." *Ellyn Plackowski, Manistique High School, Manistique, Mich.*

"Rodgers' version (the stage play) is a very faithful adaptation of Capra's classic. He obviously knows what average American community theatres are looking for. It's also broken down into very manageable segments, making rehearsals easier. Crowd appeal was very high and no one minded that our leading man looked/sounded NOTHING like Jimmy Stewart!"

Neal Lewing, Port Polson Players Theater, Polson, Mont.

ACT ONE

SCENE: *A dark and cold Christmas Eve, early evening on a bridge or near the edge of a cliff just outside the city limits of Bedford Falls. The gray cast of the lights and the sound of the wind suggest that it is snowing.*

AT RISE: *GEORGE BAILEY walks into the area. He is obviously depressed. What should appear as if out of nowhere, steps an angelic, little old man, CLARENCE. He calls out just as GEORGE is about to fling himself off into the water.*

CLARENCE. I wouldn't do it if I were you.

GEORGE. Wouldn't do what?

CLARENCE. What you were thinking of doing.

GEORGE. How do you know what I was thinking?

CLARENCE. Oh, we make it our business to know lots of things.

GEORGE. Look, whatever you're selling, I'm not interested. Please, just leave me alone?

CLARENCE. No, you don't understand. I've got a job to do here.

GEORGE. I said, leave me alone.

CLARENCE *(moving away from GEORGE and glancing up to Heaven).* This isn't going very well. *(Responding to someone above that we can neither see nor hear.)* Well, you said this was going to be easy. *(Pause for the unseen*

7

and unheard voice from above.) But he won't listen. *(Another beat.)* I know, I know. If at first you don't succeed...blah, blah, blah, blah, blah. *(Gathers his thoughts for a moment, then moves back to GEORGE.)* Have you ever read *Tom Sawyer*?

GEORGE. What?

CLARENCE. Now there was an industrious young man, and when the chips were down, he never gave up. You remember why?

GEORGE. Who cares?

CLARENCE. He kept thinking about others, George. Not about himself but about all the folks who needed him.

GEORGE. You called me George. How do you know my name?

CLARENCE. Oh, I know all about you. I've watched you grow up from a little boy.

GEORGE. How could you? I've never seen you before.

CLARENCE. You haven't needed to 'til now. How's the lip? Looks like it's stopped bleeding.

GEORGE *(sarcastically).* That's the answer I got to a prayer a little bit ago.

CLARENCE. Oh, no—no—no, George, I'm the answer to your prayer.

GEORGE. Who are you?

CLARENCE. Clarence Odbody, A-S-2.

GEORGE. Odbody...A-S-2. What's that A-S-2?

CLARENCE. Angel, Second Class.

GEORGE. Now I know I've lost my mind.

CLARENCE. Not yet. But you were well on your way. That's why they sent me down. Besides, it's ridiculous to think of killing yourself for a measly eight thousand dollars.

GEORGE. How did you know that?

CLARENCE. I've been trying to tell you. I'm your guardian angel. I know everything about you.

GEORGE. Well you look like the kind of angel I'd get, I'll give you that much. Sort of a...fallen angel. What happened to your wings?

CLARENCE. I haven't won my wings yet. That's why I'm an Angel, Second Class. But you're going to change all that.

GEORGE. I am. How?

CLARENCE. By letting me help you.

GEORGE. Only way you can help me is to get me eight thousand bucks before the clock strikes twelve. After that my life turns into a pumpkin.

CLARENCE. Sorry, but we don't use money in Heaven.

GEORGE. That's right. I keep forgetting. Well, down here you can't live without it. And if the truth be known, I'm worth a lot more dead than alive.

CLARENCE. Now look, I told you, you mustn't talk like that. I won't get my wings with that attitude. Besides, you don't realize how much you are worth. Why, if it hadn't been for you...

GEORGE. If it hadn't been for me, everybody I know would be a lot better off. Everybody. My wife, my kids, my friends.

CLARENCE. You sure have got plenty of friends, I'll say that for you. Why, do you know they've jammed up our air waves for over an hour now.

GEORGE. What are you talking about?

CLARENCE. Prayers. When they're heartfelt, they're mighty powerful missiles. And the ones for you...why, they've lit up our whole celestial system.

GEORGE. Why? How?

CLARENCE. Because you're such an important influence in so many lives, George. Always have been. Just like Tom Sawyer.

GEORGE. Since when?

CLARENCE. Ever since that day you saved your little brother from drowning when he fell through the ice.

GEORGE. That was instinct. Besides, I was only twelve.

CLARENCE. There were other boys there that day, some of them older and better swimmers. They didn't nod to their instincts. Only you did.

GEORGE. He was my brother.

CLARENCE. I know. But what about Mr. Gower when you saved *him* from ruin. That wasn't instinct. That was courage. Deep-seated and wrenched-full-of-guts courage.

GEORGE. But he had just received a telegram telling him his son had died.

CLARENCE. And he had turned mean through and through from drowning his sorrow in a bottle. Remember?

(Lights fade down but not out on GEORGE and CLARENCE. On the other side of the stage the lights come up on MR. GOWER. He is holding his hand over the mouthpiece of a candlestick phone and calling out. He is obviously quite drunk.)

GOWER. George! Are you out there? *(Into phone.)* I'm sorry, Mrs. Blaine, that medicine should have been there an hour ago. I promise you, it'll be over in five minutes. *(Hangs up the phone and turns to YOUNG GEORGE.)* Where's Mrs. Blaine's box of capsules? Why didn't you deliver them?

(During the conversation, YOUNG GEORGE has entered and stands next to MR. GOWER.)

YOUNG GEORGE. I couldn't. *(MR. GOWER grabs him by the shirt and begins hitting him about the head with his open hands. YOUNG GEORGE tries to protect himself as best he can.)*

GOWER. Why couldn't you deliver them? What kind of tricks are you playing, young man? Don't you know the Blaine boy's very sick?

YOUNG GEORGE. You're hurting my sore ear, Mr. Gower.

GOWER *(hitting him again).* You lazy loafer!

YOUNG GEORGE. Mr. Gower, you don't know what you're doing. You put something wrong in those capsules.

GOWER. What are you talking about?

YOUNG GEORGE. I know you're unhappy. You got that telegram today and it upset you. I understand that. But you put something bad in those capsules. I'm sure you did.

GOWER. How do you mean?

YOUNG GEORGE. Just look and see for yourself. *(He pulls out a box of capsules.)* I tried to tell you when you were filling the order but you wouldn't listen. But look at the bottle you took the powder from. It's not right. I swear it isn't. *(MR. GOWER grabs the box of capsules out of YOUNG GEORGE's hand, shakes the powder out of one of the capsules, and cautiously tastes it.)*

GOWER. Oh no...no...no...

YOUNG GEORGE. Don't hurt my ear again! *(MR. GOWER falls to his knees in front of him, holds him fast and begins sobbing.)* I won't tell anyone, Mr. Gower, I promise. I know what you're feeling. I won't ever tell a soul. Hope to die, I won't.

GOWER. Oh, George.

(The lights fade on YOUNG GEORGE and MR. GOWER and come back up full on CLARENCE and GEORGE on the bridge.)

CLARENCE. And you never did. Not to this day. That's remarkable.

GEORGE. He's always cared about young people. Gave lots of us our first job.

CLARENCE. Well, he never stopped caring about you, that's for sure. Remember that handsome suitcase he bought you when you thought you were finally heading off for college?

GEORGE. That was a thousand years ago.

(Lights fade up on MR. GOWER, MOTHER BAILEY, HARRY, AUNT TILLY and UNCLE BILLY, BERT and ERNIE, and VIOLET PETERSON. MR. GOWER is holding a new suitcase and they are all singing "For he's a jolly good fellow... " GEORGE walks into the picture. CLARENCE observes the scene until it is established and then exits offstage.)

GOWER. May you always use it in good health, George.

GEORGE. How can I thank you, Mr. Gower?

GOWER. By graduating with honors. That would make us all very proud.

HARRY. Fat chance.

GEORGE. Lay you a bet, little brother.

HARRY. Haven't got time. I'm off to my dance. How do I look?

GEORGE. Like a goon in a penguin suit. Where's the funeral?

MOTHER BAILEY. That's enough, you two. You look very nice, Harry.

GEORGE. Of course he does. It's my tux.

HARRY. And what's *your* verdict, Aunt Tilly? Do I look good enough to eat?

AUNT TILLY. If you lay a hand on me, young man, I'll hit you with this purse.

HARRY. Aunt Tilly, I'm in love with you and there's a full moon out tonight. *(She screams and hides behind UNCLE BILLY.)*

MOTHER BAILEY. Harry, that's enough.

HARRY. Hey, Mom, got to borrow the car. I have to take over a lot of plates and stuff.

MOTHER BAILEY. Whose plates?

HARRY. I'm chairman of the eats committee, Mom, and we're short a couple of dozen plates. *(He starts off.)*

MOTHER BAILEY *(following him out)*. Now, wait a minute, Harry, you can't use my Sunday china. It was your grandmother's and her mother's before that. Are you listening to me?

VIOLET. We are all going to miss you, George.

GEORGE. Thank you, Violet.

UNCLE BILLY. Say, that's some dress you've got on there.

VIOLET. This old thing! Why, it's just a hand-me-down, like Harry's.

UNCLE BILLY. Well, it sure is pretty, isn't it, George?

GEORGE. What? Oh, the dress. Yes, it's real nice, Violet.

VIOLET. Well, I guess I better be going. The dance starts in another half hour. Why don't you drop by later on.

GEORGE. Just might do that.

VIOLET. Hope you do. Good-bye, now.

BERT. Want Ernie and me to walk you over to the school?

VIOLET. That won't be necessary. Take care, George. *(She exits.)*

GEORGE. Yeah. You too, Violet.

BERT. Well, come on, Ernie.

ERNIE. See you around, George. *(ERNIE and BERT exit.)*

GEORGE *(turning to UNCLE BILLY)*. Say, Uncle Billy, where's Pop?

UNCLE BILLY. Had to finish up a special report for Potter. The board meeting's tomorrow.

GEORGE. I thought when Pop put him on the Board of Directors, he'd ease up on us. What's eating that old money-grabbing buzzard anyway?

AUNT TILLY. Oh, he's a sick man, George. Sick in his mind, sick in his soul, if he has one. Hates everybody who has anything that he can't have. Hates us mostly, I'm afraid.

UNCLE BILLY. After you graduate, you wouldn't consider coming back to the Building and Loan with us, would you, George?

GEORGE. Not me, Uncle Billy. I couldn't face being cooped up for the rest of my life in a shabby little office. I'm sorry, but the thought of spending all my life trying to figure out how to save three cents on a length of pipe…I'd go crazy. I want to do something big, something important.

UNCLE BILLY. Well, you know, George, I think your dad and I feel that in a small way we are doing something important. It's deep in the soul of a man to want to own his own roof and walls and a fireplace to sit beside of an evening, and we'd like to feel that we're helping him get those things.

AUNT TILLY. But, Bill, you've got to admit that this town is no place for any man unless he's willing to crawl to Potter. Now, you've got talent, George. We've all seen it. So, you go on and get yourself an education and then get out of here if you must.

UNCLE BILLY. Have any idea what you want to do, George?

GEORGE. Sure. I want to build things like skyscrapers, maybe even cities. It's been a dream all my life.

UNCLE BILLY. Still after the first million before you're thirty?

GEORGE. No. I'll settle for half that in cash.

UNCLE BILLY. Well, your Aunt Tilly and I are sure going to miss you.

GEORGE. And I'm going to miss all of you, that's for certain. *(Handing the suitcase to UNCLE BILLY.)* Do you mind taking this into the house? I think I'll walk over to the school and drop in on Harry's dance.

AUNT TILLY. Have a good time, son.

(Lights cross fade to CLARENCE who has entered unobserved near the end of the previous scene. He stays alone in this sequence. GEORGE is off stage changing costume.)

CLARENCE. And you did too. Remember? That was the night you met Mary Hatch. Of course, you had known Mary all your life. She grew up three or four years right behind you and was always there, somewhere in the background...tagging along until one of you boys noticed and sent her on her way. But that never discouraged her, not her or any of the girls. They all had their eyes hooked on you—especially Violet and Mary. You just never took the bait until Harry's graduation party. That's when you danced the Charleston all night with Mary Hatch until someone tripped the lock on the moving gym floor and everyone fell—or jumped into the swimming pool.

(Lights fade on CLARENCE and come up on GEORGE and MARY walking down a residential street. The night is warm with a bright moon. GEORGE is dressed in jersey

sweater and oversized football pants that keep wanting to come down. MARY is in an old white bathrobe. Each is carrying their wet clothes tied into a bundle. They enter singing.)

GEORGE and MARY. "Buffalo gals, can't you come out to-night, can't you come out tonight, can't you come out to-night. Buffalo gals, can't you come out tonight and dance by the light of the moon."

GEORGE. Hot dog! Just like the church choir.

MARY. Beautiful.

GEORGE. You should have seen the commotion in that locker room. I had to knock down three people to get this stuff we're wearing. I bet over half your class jumped in that pool.

MARY. Half the town said it wasn't a good idea to build the gym floor over a swimming pool. I wonder who turned the key.

GEORGE. Probably someone jealous 'cause you chose me to dance with ya.

MARY. You think, maybe?

GEORGE. Here, let me hold that old wet dress of yours. *(He takes the bundle of clothes from MARY. They stop and look at each other.)* Hello.

MARY. Hello. You look at me as if you don't know me.

GEORGE. Well, I don't.

MARY. You've passed me on the street almost every day.

GEORGE. Me?

MARY. Uh-huh.

GEORGE. Uh-uh. That was a little girl named Mary Hatch. That wasn't you.

MARY *(laughing)*. Do I look as funny as you do?

GEORGE. I guess I'm not quite the football type. You...you look wonderful. You know, if it wasn't me talking I'd say you were the prettiest girl in town.

MARY. Well, why don't you say it?

GEORGE. I don't know. Maybe I will say it. How old are you, anyway?

MARY. You can't ask that.

GEORGE. Well, I am.

MARY. Eighteen.

GEORGE. Eighteen! Why, it was only last year you were seventeen.

MARY. Too young or too old?

GEORGE. Oh, no. Just right. Your age fits you. Yes, sir, you look a little older without your clothes on. *(MARY stops. GEORGE, to cover his embarrassment, talks quickly on.)* I mean, without a dress. You look older...I mean, younger. You look just...*(In his confusion GEORGE steps on the end of the belt from MARY's robe, which is trailing along behind her. She gathers the robe around her.)* Oh-oh... sorry.

MARY. Sir, my train, please.

GEORGE. A pox upon me for a clumsy lout. *(He picks up the belt and throws it over her arm.)* Your...your caboose, my lady.

MARY. You may kiss my hand.

GEORGE. Ummmm...*(Holding her hand, GEORGE moves in closer to her.)* Uh...Mary. *(Just as he is about to kiss her, MARY turns away singing.)*

MARY. "As I was lumbering down the street..." *(GEORGE looks after her, then pantomimes picking up a rock from the street.)*

GEORGE. Okay then, I'll throw a rock at the old Granville house.

MARY. Oh, no, don't. I love that old house.

GEORGE. No. You see, you make a wish, and then try and break some glass. You got to be a pretty good shot nowadays, too, with so many windows already broken out.

MARY. Oh, no, George, don't. It's full of romance, that old place. I'd like to live in it.

GEORGE. In that old place?

MARY. Uh-huh.

GEORGE. I wouldn't live in it as a ghost. Now watch...right on the second floor there. *(GEORGE hurls the imaginary rock out over the audience. We hear the sound of a window breaking.)*

MARY. What'd you wish, George?

GEORGE. Well, not just one wish. A whole hat full, Mary. I know what I'm going to do tomorrow and the next day and the next year and the year after that. I'm shaking the dust of this crummy little town off my feet and I'm going to see the world. Italy, Greece, the Parthenon, the Coliseum. Then I'm going to go to college and see what they know...and then I'm going to build things. I'm gonna build air fields, and I'm going to build skyscrapers a hundred stories high. I'm gonna build bridges a mile long...*(As he talks, MARY has been listening intently. She finally stoops down and picks up an imaginary rock, weighing it in her hand.)* Are you gonna throw a rock? *(MARY throws her imaginary rock, and once more we hear the sound of breaking glass.)* Hey, that's pretty good. What'd you wish, Mary? *(MARY looks at him provocatively, then turns, and shuffles off down the street, singing as she goes. GEORGE hurries after her.)*

MARY. "Buffalo gals, can't you come out tonight..." *(GEORGE catches up with her, takes her hand, and joins in singing.)*

GEORGE and MARY.) "...can't you come out tonight, can't you come out tonight. Buffalo gals, can't you come out tonight and dance by the light of the moon."

GEORGE. What did you wish when you threw that rock?

MARY *(turns and looks up at GEORGE)*. Oh, no.

GEORGE. Come on, tell me.

MARY. If I told you it might not come true.

GEORGE. What is it you want, Mary? You want the moon? Just say the word and I'll throw a lasso around it and pull it down. Hey, that's a pretty good idea. I'll give you the moon, Mary

MARY. I'll take it. And then what?

GEORGE. Well, then you could swallow it and it'd all dissolve, see? And the moonbeams'd shoot out of your fingers and your toes, and the ends of your hair. *(Pause.)* Am I talking too much?

(During the latter part of this conversation, BERT and ERNIE walk on and watch GEORGE and MARY.)

BERT. Yes, you are!!

GEORGE. Who's that?

ERNIE. Why don't you kiss her instead of talking her to death?

GEORGE. What?

BERT *(as he walks past them and exits, teasing)*. Aw, youth. You know, it's wasted on the wrong people, Ernie.

ERNIE. You're telling me.

BERT. Just wasted! *(They exit.)*

GEORGE *(calling after them)*. Hey, hey, hold on. Bert, Ernie, come on back here. I'll show you some kissing that will turn your head around.

(At the opposite side of the stage, UNCLE BILLY comes rushing on stage.)

UNCLE BILLY. George! George! Come on home, quick! Your father's had a stroke!

GEORGE. Pop? Mary, I'm sorry. I've got to go.

UNCLE BILLY. Come on, George, let's hurry.

GEORGE *(as he crosses to UNCLE BILLY)*. Did you send for a doctor?

UNCLE BILLY. Yes, Campbell's there now.

(GEORGE and UNCLE BILLY exit. MARY stands alone for a moment. Off stage, a solo voice, or a small ensemble, begins singing, a cappella, an appropriate hymn. MARY exits as AUNT TILLY and UNCLE BILLY lead MRS. BAILEY, HARRY, and a group of mourners on stage. HENRY F. POTTER, accompanied by his SECRETARY, is rolled in in his wheelchair by his GOON, but stays somewhat apart from the rest of the group. MRS. BAILEY kneels and prays over an imaginary grave. During this part of the ritual [and when they have completed a costume change], MARY and GEORGE enter on opposite sides of the stage. MARY joins her mother and GEORGE stays in the background. Everyone exits leaving only GEORGE, and MR. POTTER with his GOON and SECRETARY. GEORGE crosses to MR. POTTER.)

GEORGE. It was nice of you to come, Mr. Potter.

POTTER. Well, I'd say your father *was* the Building and Loan here in Bedford Falls, George.

GEORGE. I agree, Mr. Potter.

POTTER. Of course, he wasn't a businessman and that's what killed him. Oh, I don't mean any disrespect, George, God rest his soul. He was a man of high ideals...so called, but ideals without common sense can ruin this town. So, at our next Board of Trustees meeting I'm going to make a motion.

GEORGE. A motion?

POTTER. That's right. A motion to dissolve the institution and turn its assets and liabilities over to receivership.

GEORGE. But, Mr. Potter...

POTTER (holding up several legal size papers stapled together). Take this loan application the Board's to act on this morning...to Ernie Bishop. You know, that fellow walks around all day and delivers our mail...usually late because he's always stopping to talk to everyone on his route...well, anyway, I happen to know that the bank turned down his loan, but he came to the Building and Loan and we're willing to build him a house worth five thousand dollars. Why?

GEORGE. Well, I handled that, Mr. Potter. You have all the papers there. His salary, insurance, and I can personally vouch for his character.

POTTER (sarcastically). Oh, he's a friend of yours?

GEORGE. Yes, sir.

POTTER. So, if you shoot pool with the manager's son, you can borrow money. And what does it get the Building and Loan? A discontented, lazy rabble instead of a thrifty, working class. And all because a few starry-eyed dreamers like your father stir them up and fill their heads with a lot of impossible ideas.

GEORGE. Just a minute—just a minute. Now, hold on, Mr. Potter. You're right when you say my father was no businessman. I know that. Why he ever started this cheap, penny-ante Building and Loan, I'll never know. But neither you nor anybody else can say anything against his character, because his whole life was...Why, in the twenty-five years since he and Uncle Billy started the institution, he never once thought of himself or saved any money. But he *did* help a few people get out of your slums, Mr. Potter. And what's wrong with that? Just remember this, the rabble you're talking about...they do most of the working and paying and living and dying in this community. Well, is it too much to have them work and pay and live and die in a couple of decent rooms and a bath? My father didn't think so. People were human beings to him, but to you, a warped, frustrated old man, they're cattle. Well, in my book, my father died a much richer man than you'll ever be!

POTTER. I'm not interested in your book, young man. I'm talking about the Building and Loan.

GEORGE. I know very well what you're talking about. You're talking about something you can't get your fingers on, and it's galling you. That's what you're talking about. Well, thank you for stopping by, Mr. Potter. I'll see you at the meeting.

POTTER. But you're not on the Board.

GEORGE. I hold my father's proxy so I can attend. And cast a vote. You see, the way I look at it, Mr. Potter, the people of this town need our family's one-horse institution if only to have some place where they can go without crawling to you.

POTTER *(to his GOON)*. Get me out of here. *(To GEORGE as he is being rolled off.)* Sentimental hogwash! I'm still going to make my motion, young man, and we'll see who has the power in this town.

(CLARENCE enters the circle of light where GEORGE is standing.)

CLARENCE. But you spoke eloquently at the board meeting that day and they voted Potter down, remember?

GEORGE. But on one condition I hadn't banked on.

CLARENCE. That you take over your father's place. And you did. And you turned over all your school money to your brother Harry and sent him to college.

GEORGE (with pride). And Harry became a football star—made second team All-American.

CLARENCE. And you—you got four years older.

(CLARENCE disappears out of the light again as GEORGE looks out wishfully. After a moment, MOTHER BAILEY enters from behind, crosses down to GEORGE, and kisses him on the cheek.)

MOTHER BAILEY. That's for nothing.

GEORGE. Hello, Mom.

MOTHER BAILEY. What're you doing? Wishing on the moon?

GEORGE. No, I've given up on that. Just getting some air.

MOTHER BAILEY. Did you know that Mary Hatch is back from school?

GEORGE. Uh-huh.

MOTHER BAILEY. Came back three days ago.

GEORGE (playing along with her game). Hmmmm...

MOTHER BAILEY. Nice girl, Mary.

GEORGE. Hmmmm...

MOTHER BAILEY. Kind that will help you find the answers, George.

GEORGE. Hmmmm...

MOTHER BAILEY. Can you give me one good reason why you shouldn't call on Mary?

GEORGE. Sure—Sam Wainwright.

MOTHER BAILEY (knowingly). Hmmmm...

GEORGE. Yes, Sam's crazy about Mary.

MOTHER BAILEY. Well, she's not crazy about him.

GEORGE. Well, how do you know? Did she discuss it with you?

MOTHER BAILEY. No.

GEORGE. Well, how do you know then?

MOTHER BAILEY. Well, I've got eyes, haven't I? Why, she lights up like a firefly whenever you're around.

GEORGE. Oh...

MOTHER BAILEY. And besides, Sam Wainwright's away in New York, and you're here in Bedford Falls.

GEORGE. And all's fair in love and war?

MOTHER BAILEY (teasing, still playing the game). Well, I don't know about war.

GEORGE. Mother, you know, I can see right through you— right to your back collar button...trying to get rid of me, huh?

MOTHER BAILEY. Uh-huh. (They kiss. MOTHER BAILEY puts GEORGE's hat on his head.)

GEORGE. Well, here's your hat, what's your hurry? All right, Mother, old Building and Loan pal, if you insist, I'll go out and find a girl and do a little passionate necking.

MOTHER BAILEY. George!

GEORGE. Now if you'll just point me in the right direction... This direction? (As he leaves.) Good night, Mrs. Bailey.

(As GEORGE crosses R, MOTHER BAILEY exits out of the light, U. When GEORGE gets RC he stops and just stands, hands in his pockets, obviously undecided as to what he wants to do. VIOLET enters.)

VIOLET. Hello, Georgie-Porgie.

GEORGE. Hello, Vi. How's business at Ye Old-fashioned Permanent Wave Shoppe?

VIOLET. Not a tidal wave yet, but I'm getting some city mothers in—thanks to you. What gives with you?

GEORGE. Nothing.

VIOLET. Where are you going?

GEORGE. Oh, I'll probably end up down at the library.

VIOLET. Georgie, don't you ever get tired of just reading about things? *(Her eyes are seductive and guileful as she looks up at him. He is silent for a moment.)*

GEORGE *(blurts out)*. Yes...yes, I do. What are you doing tonight?

VIOLET *(feigned surprise)*. Not a thing.

GEORGE. Are you game, Vi? Let's make a night of it.

VIOLET *(just what she wanted)*. Oh, I'd love it, Georgie. What'll we do?

GEORGE. Let's go out in the field and take off our shoes and walk through the grass.

VIOLET. Huh?

GEORGE. Then we can climb Mount Bedford, up to the falls and smell the pines, and watch the sunrise against the peaks, and...we'll stay up there the whole night, and everybody'll be talking and there'll be a terrific scandal...

VIOLET *(interrupting)*. Walk in the grass in my bare feet? George, have you gone crazy? And Mount Bedford. Who would want to climb all the way to the top of Mount Bed ford? It's got to be a ten-mile hike at least.

GEORGE. Okay, forget the whole thing. It was just a crazy idea.

VIOLET. You're telling me. Good night, George.

(VIOLET exits stage R. GEORGE continues to stand where he is for a few more seconds, obviously debating with him-

self. Then he slowly walks stage L. When he gets there, MARY steps out into the light from U.)

MARY. Well, there you are.

GEORGE. Hello, Mary. I just happened to be passing by.

MARY. Yes, so I noticed. Have you made up your mind?

GEORGE. How's that?

MARY. Have you made up your mind?

GEORGE. About what?

MARY. Paying a visit. Your mother phoned and said you were on your way over.

GEORGE. My mother called you? Well, how did she know?

MARY. Didn't you tell her?

GEORGE. I didn't tell anybody. I just went for a walk and happened to be passing by...

(At this point a wagon—the front porch of the Hatch's home—rolls on. It displays a screened front door and an open window. On the U side of the window is a small table holding a candlestick phone.)

MARY. Well, do you want to come up on the porch and sit a minute?

GEORGE. Well, maybe for a minute, but I didn't tell anybody I was coming over here. *(They stand there, looking at each other for a moment.)* When did you get back?

MARY. Tuesday.

GEORGE. Where'd you get that dress?

MARY. Do you like it?

GEORGE. It's okay. I thought you'd go back to New York like Sam and Ingie, and the rest of them.

MARY. Oh, I worked there a couple of vacations, but I don't know...I guess I was homesick.

GEORGE (*shocked*). Homesick? For Bedford Falls?

MARY. Yes, and my family and…oh, everything. Aren't you coming up on the porch?

GEORGE. Well, maybe just for a minute. But I want you to know that I didn't tell anybody that I was coming here.

MARY. Would you rather leave?

GEORGE (*jumping on this*). No!…(*Now trying to be casual.*) I mean, I don't want to be rude.

MARY. Then, come on up. (*They move up on the porch. MARY sits on the top step. GEORGE remains standing. An awkward moment of silence. Then MARY starts singing quietly.*) "Buffalo gals, won't you come out tonight, come out tonight, come out tonight…" (*GEORGE joins in and together they finish the chorus.*)

GEORGE and MARY. "Buffalo gals, can't you come out tonight and dance by the light of the moon."

MRS. HATCH'S VOICE. Mary! Mary, who's down there with you?

MARY. It's George Bailey, Mother.

MRS. HATCH'S VOICE. George Bailey! What does he want?

MARY. I don't know. (*To GEORGE.*) What do you want?

GEORGE. Me? Not a thing.

MARY. He's making violent love to me, Mother.

MRS. HATCH'S VOICE. You tell him to go right back home, and don't you leave the house, either. Sam Wainwright promised to call you from New York tonight. (*Phone rings.*) There he is now. Good night, George.

GEORGE. I better be going. (*Starts to leave.*)

MARY. No! Wait a minute.

MRS. HATCH'S VOICE. Mary, get the phone.

MARY *(into phone).* Hello. Sam, how are you? Guess who's here. George Bailey. George! It's Sam. He wants to talk to you.

GEORGE. Me?

MARY. Hurry. It's long distance.

GEORGE. Hello, Sam?

(A light comes up on SAM WAINWRIGHT on the opposite side of the stage.)

SAM. Well, George Baileyoffski! Hey, a fine pal you are. What are you trying to do? Steal my girl?

GEORGE. What do you mean? Nobody's trying to steal your girl. Here...here's Mary.

SAM. No, wait a minute. Wait a minute. I want to talk to both of you. Tell Mary to get on the extension.

GEORGE. He wants you to get on the extension.

MARY. Mother's on the extension. *(She steps in closer to GEORGE, puts her hand below his on the phone.)* Now we can both hear. *(On phone).* We're listening, Sam.

SAM. I have a big deal coming up that's going to make us all rich. George, you remember that night in Martini's bar when you told me you read someplace about making plastics out of soybeans?

GEORGE. Huh? Yeah-yeah-yeah...soybeans. Sure.

SAM. Well, Dad snapped up the idea. He's going to build a factory outside of Rochester. And here's the point. Mary? Mary, you're in on this too. Now listen. George, have you got any money.

GEORGE. Money? Yeah...well, a little.

SAM. Well, now listen up. I want you to put every cent you've got into our stocks, you hear? And George, I may have a job for you, that is, unless you're still married to that broken-down Building and Loan. This is the biggest thing since radio, and I'm letting you in on the ground floor. Oh, Mary…Mary…

MARY *(nervously)*. I'm here.

SAM. Would you tell that guy I'm giving him the chance of a lifetime, you hear? The chance of a lifetime. *(As MARY listens, she turns to look at GEORGE, her lips almost on his lips.)*

MARY. He says it's the chance of a lifetime. *(GEORGE can stand it no longer. He drops the phone with a crash, grabs MARY by the shoulders and shakes her.)*

GEORGE *(fiercely)*. Now you listen to me! I don't want any plastics! I don't want any ground floors, and I don't want to get married—ever—to anyone! You understand that? I want to do what I want to do. And you're…*(He pulls her to him in a fierce embrace.)* Oh, Mary…Mary…

MARY. George…George.

(They kiss. We hear the sound of the "Wedding March." The Hatch's front parlor wagon rolls off as the TOWNS-PEOPLE rush on as if waiting for the bride and groom to enter out of a church. As GEORGE and MARY come forward everyone applauds and shouts congratulations. MRS. BAILEY, UNCLE BILLY and AUNT TILLY are on one side of the couple, MRS. HATCH on the other. ERNIE steps forward and hands GEORGE a bottle of champagne done up in gift wrapping.)

ERNIE. Bert and I chipped in on this. We hope you float away to Happy Land on the bubbles.

GEORGE. Oh, look at this. Champagne!

MARY. Thank you, Ernie.

ERNIE. By the way, where are you two going on this here-now honeymoon?

GEORGE. Where are we going? *(Takes out a fat roll of bills.)* Look at this. There's the kitty, Ernie. Here, come on, count it, Mary.

MARY. I feel like a bootlegger's wife. *(Holding up the money.)* Look!

GEORGE. You know what we're going to do? We're going to shoot the works. A whole week in New York. A whole week in Bermuda. The highest hotels—the oldest champagne—the richest caviar—the hottest music, and the prettiest wife!

ERNIE. That does it! Then what?

GEORGE *(to MARY)*. Then what, honey?

MARY. After that, who cares?

GEORGE. That does it—come here.

(They kiss. The TOWNSFOLK applaud. BERT rushes in.)

BERT. I hate to break anything up but there's something funny going on down at the bank. I've never really seen one, but it has all the earmarks of a run.

MRS. MARTINI. Oh, my God.

BERT. If you got any money in the bank, folks, you better hurry. *(The TOWNSFOLK all react in panic and run off.)*

GEORGE. You wait here, dear. I'll be just a minute. *(He starts to exit.)*

MARY. George, let's not stop. Please, let's go.

GEORGE. I'll be back in a minute, Mary.

(The lights come up on the Building and Loan wagon as it is rolled in. UNCLE BILLY and AUNT TILLY are present. UNCLE BILLY is sneaking a drink from his flask.

GEORGE crosses into the scene, MARY exits. GEORGE pulls UNCLE BILLY downstage as the TOWNSPEOPLE rush in and jam up at the deposit cage. The group should include ERNIE, BERT, MR. MARTINI, MR. WELCH, MRS. MARTINI, MISS CARTER, MISS ANDREWS and MRS. THOMPSON. Note: If you want more people in the scene, you could have MRS. BAILEY, MRS. HATCH, VIOLET and MR. POTTER's SECRETARY enter and observe. The actors playing HARRY and SAM could also be in the scene, not as their character but as a townsperson.)

GEORGE. What's the meaning of this, Uncle Billy? A holiday?

UNCLE BILLY. This is what you call a pickle, George, a real pickle.

GEORGE. All right now, what happened? How did it start?

UNCLE BILLY. How does anything like this ever start? All I know is the bank called our loan.

GEORGE. When?

UNCLE BILLY. About an hour ago. I had to hand over all our cash.

GEORGE. All of it?

UNCLE BILLY. Every cent of it, and it still was less than we owe.

GEORGE. Holy mackerel!

UNCLE BILLY. The whole town's gone crazy.

(At this moment POTTER is wheeled in by his GOON.)

GEORGE. Mr. Potter. To what do we owe this unexpected visit?

POTTER. George, there's a rumor around town that you're going to close your doors early. Is that true?

GEORGE (*checking his watch*). Not for another ten minutes. That's our regular closing time.

POTTER. Well, I'm glad to hear that…George, are you all right? Do you want me to call the sheriff?

GEORGE. What for?

POTTER. Well, mobs get pretty ugly sometimes, you know.

GEORGE. I can assure you, all of our customers are very polite.

POTTER. I'm sure. George, I'm going all out to help in this crisis. I've just guaranteed the bank sufficient funds to meet their needs. They'll close down for a week, and then reopen.

GEORGE. You've taken over the bank?

POTTER. I may lose a fortune, but I'm willing to guarantee your people too. (*To the TOWNSPEOPLE.*) Just bring your shares over to the bank and I will pay fifty cents on the dollar.

GEORGE. I'm sure that won't be necessary, Mr. Potter. We'll take care of our customers right here.

POTTER. Well, just make sure you don't close your doors before six p.m. or you'll never reopen. (*He motions to his GOON who turns and wheels him out.*) Ladies. Gentlemen. Remember, fifty cents on the dollar.

GEORGE (*calling after him*). You never miss a trick, do you, Potter? Well, you're going to miss this one. (*The TOWNS-PEOPLE push to line up at the teller window.*) Now don't panic, folks. You heard Mr. Potter. The bank will open in a week.

MISS ANDREWS. But I've got my money here, George, and I'll take it now.

GEORGE. No. Miss Andrews, you're thinking of this place all wrong. As if I had the money back in the safe. The money's not here. Your money's in the Grange's house right next to yours. And in the Kennedy house, and Mrs. Macklin's house, and a hundred others. Why, you're lending them the money to build, and then, they're going to pay it back to you as best they can. Now what are you going to do? Foreclose on them?

MISS ANDREWS. I got two hundred and forty-two dollars in here, George Bailey, and two hundred and forty-two dollars isn't going to break anybody.

GEORGE (handing her a slip). All right, Miss Andrews, all right. Here you are. You sign this. You'll get your money in sixty days.

MISS ANDREWS. Sixty days?

GEORGE. Well, now that's what you agreed to when you bought your shares. (MISS ANDREWS starts to leave.) Now, come on, Miss Andrews, stick to your original agreement. Give us sixty days on this.

MRS. THOMPSON (to MISS ANDREWS). Are you going to go to Potter's?

MISS ANDREWS. Better to get half than nothing. (Strong reaction in agreement from the TOWNSPEOPLE.)

GEORGE. Miss Andrews! Mrs. Thompson! Wait, please... Now listen...listen to me. If Potter gets hold of this Building and Loan there'll never be another decent house built in this town. He's already got charge of the bank. He's got the bus line. He's got the department stores. And now he's after us. Why? Because we're cutting in on his business, that's why. And because he wants to keep you living in his slums and paying the kind of rent he decides. Well, we can't let him. We can get through this thing but we've got to stick together. We've got to have faith in each other.

MRS. THOMPSON. But my husband hasn't worked in over a year, and I need money.

MARTINI. How am I going to live until the bank opens?

MRS. MARTINI. We've got doctor bills to pay.

ERNIE. Yes, George, I need cash.

BERT. Can't feed my kids on faith.

(*During this scene MARY has come up behind the counter. Suddenly, as the people once more start moving toward the door, she holds up a roll of bills.*)

MARY (*calling out*). How much do you need?

GEORGE (*takes the money from MARY*). Hey, that's right. I've got two thousand dollars! Here's two thousand dollars. This'll tide us over until the bank reopens. All right, Miss Andrews, how much do you need?

MISS ANDREWS. Two hundred and forty-two dollars!

GEORGE. Aw, Miss Andrews, please, just enough to tide you over 'til the bank reopens.

MISS ANDREWS. I'll take two hundred and forty-two dollars. (*GEORGE starts rapidly to count out the money. MISS ANDREWS throws her passbook on the counter.*)

GEORGE. There you are.

MISS ANDREWS. That'll close my account.

GEORGE. Your account's still here. That's a loan. (*MISS ANDREWS moves away. So do some others, quietly and assured. ERNIE moves up to the window.*) Okay. All right, Ernie?

ERNIE. I got three hundred dollars here, George.

GEORGE. Aw, now, Ernie...what'll it take 'til the bank reopens? What do you need?

ERNIE. Well, I suppose twenty dollars.

GEORGE. Twenty dollars. Now you're talking. Fine. Thanks, Ernie. (*To MRS. THOMPSON who is next in line.*) All right, now, Mrs. Thompson. How much do you want?

MRS. THOMPSON. But it's your own money, George.

GEORGE. Never mind about that. How much do you want?

MRS. THOMPSON. I can get along with twenty, all right.

GEORGE *(counting it out).* Twenty dollars.

MRS. THOMPSON. And I'll sign a paper.

GEORGE. You don't have to sign anything. I know you'll pay it back when you can. That's okay. *(To MRS. MAR- TINI who is next in line.)* All right, Mrs. Martini.

MRS. MARTINI. Could we have seventeen-fifty?

GEORGE. Seven...*(He kisses her.)* Bless your heart. Of course you can have it. You got fifty cents? *(Handing the money over to UNCLE BILLY.)* Here you take over.

UNCLE BILLY. I think we're going to make it, George. I think we're going to make it.

GEORGE. So do I. *(GEORGE crosses downstage to MARY. The lights fade down on the teller window. All the TOWNS- PEOPLE leave by the end of the following short scene.)* Hello, Mrs. Bailey.

MARY. Hello, Mr. Bailey. How's business?

GEORGE. Booming. *(They smile at each other.)*

MARY *(holding up a key on a ring).* Well, at least you have a place to come home to. Most of the windows are broken out and the roof leaks in a place or two, but the structure's sound and there isn't a crack in the foundation.

GEORGE. What are you talking about?

MARY. Thirty-two Sycamore.

GEORGE. Thirty-two Sycamore? But that's...*(MARY nods.)*

MARY. Remember the night we broke the windows? That's what I wished for and I've been saving ever since. Happy Anniversary.

GEORGE. Happy Anniversary? We've only been married an hour.

MARY (*looking down at her watch*). One hour, twenty-nine minutes and forty some odd seconds to be exact. Soon enough to celebrate I would say. Wouldn't you?

GEORGE. Oh, darling, you're wonderful.

(*They kiss. A town clock is heard striking six p.m. Lights come back up on the Building and Loan wagon. All the TOWNSPEOPLE are gone.*)

UNCLE BILLY (*counting out the hours*). Four...five...six. Bingo! We made it. (*AUNT TILLY, GEORGE and MARY send up a cheer.*) Look, George, we're still in business. We've got two bucks left!

GEORGE. Well, pop the champagne. I'd say we're a couple of financial wizards.

UNCLE BILLY. Those Rockefellers!

GEORGE. Open the safe for these great big important simoleons.

UNCLE BILLY. We'll save them for seed.

GEORGE. Here's to Papa Dollar and to Mama Dollar, and if you want the old Building and Loan to stay in business, you better have a family real quick.

AUNT TILLY. I wish they were rabbits.

GEORGE. That's great, Aunt Tilly. Did you hear that, Uncle Billy? Rabbits. Here's to the Rabbits. (*They all raise their glasses and cry out "Rabbits." Everyone laughs and embraces as the lights fade.*)

END OF ACT ONE

ACT TWO

AT RISE: *The lights come up on GEORGE and MARY who are standing on the front stoop of one of their new homes. The Martini family and friends are standing below, their backs to the audience, listening.*

MARY *(to MRS. MARTINI, giving her a loaf of bread).* Bread! That this house may never know hunger. *(Giving her a box of salt.)* Salt! That life may always have flavor.

GEORGE *(handing a bottle of wine to MARTINI).* And wine! That joy and prosperity may reign forever. Enter the Martini castle!

(The MARTINIS and all their friends ad-lib with great enthusiasm. MRS. MARTINI hugs MARY and MR. MARTINI shakes GEORGE's hand. Lights cross fade to Potter's office. POTTER is seated in his wheelchair at his desk, with his GOON beside him. He is speaking to his bank examiner, MISS CARTER.)

MISS CARTER. You can't dismiss this Bailey Park anymore, Mr. Potter. It's cutting deeper and deeper into your rental profits.

POTTER. The Bailey family has been a boil on my neck long enough.

(MR. POTTER's SECRETARY enters.)

SECRETARY. Mr. Bailey has just arrived, sir.

POTTER. Good. Tell him to wait. *(The SECRETARY exits. To MISS CARTER.)* Go on.

MISS CARTER. As you know, he's built up a whole sub-division out next to the cemetery. Dozens and dozens of the prettiest little homes you ever saw. I'm thinking seriously of purchasing one myself.

POTTER. Don't you dare.

MISS CARTER. The point is, Mr. Potter, ninety per cent of the residents used to pay rent to you. Now if I were you, Mr. Potter...

POTTER *(interrupting)*. Well, you are not me.

MISS CARTER *(as she leaves)*. As I say, I'm just a lowly bank examiner, but if you're not careful, one of these days...

POTTER. I'm a busy man, Miss Carter. I haven't got time for idle conjecture. Good day. *(MISS CARTER exits.)* Cut into my revenue will you? Well, I'll show you a trick or two, Mr. Bailey.

(POTTER pushes the buzzer on his desk. The SECRETARY rushes into the room.)

SECRETARY. Yes, sir?

POTTER. Send Bailey in.

SECRETARY. Right away, sir. Mr. Bailey, Mr. Potter will see you now.

GEORGE. Thank you.

(GEORGE walks into the scene.)

POTTER *(with artificial warmth)*. Good morning, George. So good to see you again. *(He extends his hand.)*

GEORGE *(shaking POTTER's hand).* Mr. Potter. This is quite an unusual request.

POTTER. What's that?

GEORGE. Your calling to ask me to pay you a visit.

POTTER. Don't know what's so unusual about it. I just thought the two of us should get better acquainted. Here, have a cigar.

GEORGE. Thank you, sir. *(Inspecting the large cigar.)* This is quite a cigar.

POTTER. You like it? I'll send you a box.

GEORGE *(nervously).* Well, I...I suppose I'll find out sooner or later, but just what exactly did you want to see me about?

POTTER *(laughs).* Now that's just what I like so much about you. *(Pleasantly and smoothly.)* George, I'm an old man, and most people hate me. But I don't like them either, so that makes it all even. You know just as well as I do, that I run practically everything in this town but the Bailey Building and Loan. You know, also, that for a number of years I've been trying to get control of it...or kill it. But I haven't been able to do it. You have been stopping me. In fact, you have beaten me, George, and as anyone in this county can tell you, that takes some doing. Take during the depression, for instance. You and I were the only ones that kept our heads. You saved the Building and Loan, and I saved all the rest.

GEORGE. Yes. Well, most people say you stole all the rest.

POTTER. The envious ones say that, George, the suckers. Now, I have stated my side very frankly. Let's look at your side. Young man, twenty-seven, twenty-eight...married, making, say...forty a week.

GEORGE *(indignantly).* Forty-five!

POTTER. Forty-five. Forty-five. Out of which, after supporting your wife and your mother, and paying your bills, you're able to keep, say ten, if you skimp. A child or two comes along, and you won't even be able to save the ten. Now, if this young man of twenty-eight was a common, ordinary yokel, I'd say he was doing fine. But, George Bailey is not a common, ordinary yokel. He's an intelligent, smart, ambitious young man—who hates his job—who hates the Building and Loan, almost as much as I do. A young man who's been dying to get out on his own ever since he was born. A young man...the smartest one of the crowd, mind you, a young man who has to sit by and watch his friends go places, because he's trapped. Yes, sir, trapped into frittering his life away playing nursemaid to a lot of garlic-eaters. Do I paint a correct picture, or do I exaggerate?

GEORGE (*mystified*). Now what's your point, Mr. Potter?

POTTER. My point? My point is, I want to hire you.

GEORGE (*dumbfounded*). Hire me?

POTTER. I want you to manage my affairs, run my properties. George, I'll start you out at twenty thousand dollars a year.

GEORGE (*drops his cigar*). Twenty thou...twenty thousand dollars a year?

POTTER. You wouldn't mind living in the nicest house in town, buying your wife a lot of fine clothes, a couple of business trips to New York a year, maybe once in a while Europe. You wouldn't mind that, would you, George?

GEORGE. Would I? (*Looking around skeptically.*) You're not talking to somebody else around here, are you? You know, this is me, you remember me? George Bailey.

POTTER. Oh, yes, George Bailey. Whose ship has just come in—providing he has the brains enough to climb aboard.

GEORGE. Well, what about the Building and Loan?

POTTER. Oh, confound it, man, are you afraid of success? I'm offering you a three year contract starting at twenty thousand dollars a year. Is it a deal or isn't it?

GEORGE. Well, Mr. Potter, I...I...I know, I ought to jump at the chance, but I...I just...I wonder if it would be possible for you to give me twenty-four hours to think it over?

POTTER. Sure, sure. You go on home and talk it over with your wife.

GEORGE. I'd like to do that.

POTTER. In the meantime, I'll draw up the papers.

GEORGE. All right, sir.

POTTER (*extending his hand to GEORGE*). Okay, George.

GEORGE (*taking his hand*). Okay, Mr. Potter. (*As they shake hands, GEORGE feels a physical revulsion. POTTER's hand feels like a cold mackerel to him. In that moment of physical contact he knows he could never be associated with this man. GEORGE drops his hand with a shudder. He peers intently into POTTER's face.*) No...no...no...no, now wait a minute, here! I don't have to talk to anybody! I know right now, and the answer is no! NO! Doggone it! (*Getting madder all the time.*) You sit around here and you spin your little webs and you think the whole world revolves around you and your money. Well, it doesn't, Mr. Potter! In the...in the whole vast configuration of things, I'd say you were nothing but a scurvy little spider. You... (*He turns and shouts at the GOON, impassive as ever beside POTTER's wheelchair.*)...and that goes for you too! (*As GEORGE opens the office door to exit, he shouts at the SECRETARY who is passing him on her way in.*) And it goes for you too!

(GEORGE walks downstage out of Potter's office area. Lights cross fade: up on MARY as she crosses down to GEORGE, down on Potter's office.)

MARY *(upbeat).* Hi.

GEORGE *(still upset, downbeat).* Hi.

MARY. Been a rough day? *(GEORGE mumbles something incoherent. MARY starts singing to cheer him up.)* "Buffalo gals, won't you come out tonight, won't you come out tonight, won't you come out tonight."

GEORGE. Mary Hatch, why in the world did you ever marry a guy like me?

MARY. To keep from being an old maid.

GEORGE. You could have married Sam Wainwright or anybody else in town.

MARY. I didn't want to marry anybody else in town. I want my baby to look like you.

GEORGE. You didn't even have a honeymoon. I promise you...*(Does a double take.)*...Your what?

MARY. My baby.

GEORGE. You mean...Mary, are you on the nest?

MARY. In a manner of speaking.

GEORGE. What is it, a boy or a girl? *(MARY nods her head happily and kisses him.)*

(Lights come up on CLARENCE on the opposite side of the stage.)

CLARENCE. You were on top of the world then, George Bailey. Couldn't have been happier. *(GEORGE breaks his embrace with MARY and moves across stage to CLARENCE. MARY exits and lights fade in that area.)*

GEORGE. But that was nearly ten years ago. We've gone through a war since then.

CLARENCE. Yes, and your wife has given birth to not one but four beautiful children. And your brother, Harry, has been decorated with the Congressional Medal of Honor. "President Decorates Harry Bailey."

GEORGE. That was the headline in this morning's paper.

CLARENCE. That's right. This morning, George, day before Christmas, about ten a.m. That's when it all started, wasn't it? You were out buying a Christmas wreath *(GEORGE exits at this point.)* and Uncle Billy...oh yes, Uncle Billy was on his way to the bank.

(A YOUNG BOY selling newspapers enters.)

YOUNG BOY *(calling out).* Extra! Extra! Read all about it. Local boy wins Congressional Medal of Honor. Harry Bailey to be decorated by President.

(UNCLE BILLY enters thumbing through the bills in a thick envelope as he walks across stage. On the opposite side of the stage POTTER is wheeled in by his GOON. Lights fade out on CLARENCE.)

POTTER *(to the YOUNG BOY).* Here, give me one of those. *(POTTER grabs one of the newspapers from the YOUNG BOY. The GOON gives the BOY the money. POTTER comments on the news with disgust.)* One of those Bailey boys, again.

UNCLE BILLY *(meeting up with POTTER and his GOON).* Well, good morning, Mr. Potter. What's the news? *(He grabs the paper from POTTER's hand.)* Well, well, well, Harry Bailey wins Congressional Medal. That couldn't be one of the Bailey boys, could it? You just can't keep those Baileys down now, can you, Mr. Potter?

POTTER. How does slacker George feel about that?

UNCLE BILLY. Very jealous, oh yes, very jealous. He only lost three buttons off his vest. Of course, slacker George would have gotten two of those medals if he had been allowed to go.

POTTER. I know, he has a bad ear.

UNCLE BILLY. That's right. *(He folds POTTER's paper over the envelope containing his money and flings his final taunt at the old man.)* After all, Potter, some people like George had to stay home. Not every heel was in Germany and Japan!

POTTER. Give me back my paper. Buy your own if you want to drool over it. *(In a cold rage, POTTER grabs his paper, and is pushed across to stage R by his GOON. UNCLE BILLY laughs as he exits L singing " 'Tis the season to be jolly... " When POTTER reaches stage R he realizes that an envelope has been folded up in his paper. To his GOON.)* Wait a minute. *(He examines the contents of the envelope and realizes that it is full of money. He turns and starts to call off after UNCLE BILLY.)* Hey! *(To himself.)* No. Wait a minute. *(Looking at the money.)* Why not. Yes, why not. *(To the GOON.)* Hurry, take me straight to the bank.

(Lights fade on POTTER as he is wheeled off and come up on the front room of the Bailey Building and Loan. AUNT TILLY is talking on the phone. MISS CARTER is seated on a chair. She is holding a briefcase. GEORGE enters, holding up a newspaper and carrying a Christmas wreath.)

GEORGE *(with great pride)*. Extra! Extra! Read all about it!

AUNT TILLY *(on the phone)*. George! George! It's Harry now on long distance from Washington.!

GEORGE. Harry! What do you know about that?

AUNT TILLY. He reversed the charges. It's okay, isn't it?

GEORGE. What do you mean is it okay? For a hero? *(Takes the phone.)* Harry! Oh, you old seven-kinds of a son-of-a-gun. Congratulations! How's Mother standing it?...She did? What do you know...*(To AUNT TILLY.)* Mother had lunch with the President's wife.

AUNT TILLY. Wait 'til Bill hears about this. *(To GEORGE.)* What did they have to eat?

GEORGE *(on phone)*. What did they have to eat? Harry, you should see what they're cooking up in the town for you...Oh, are they? *(To AUNT TILLY.)* The Navy's going to fly Mother home this afternoon.

AUNT TILLY. In a plane?

GEORGE *(on phone)*. What? Uncle Billy? *(To AUNT TILLY.)* Has Uncle Billy come in yet?

AUNT TILLY. No, he stopped at the bank first.

GEORGE *(on phone)*. He's not here right now, Harry. But look...

AUNT TILLY *(interrupting)*. George...

GEORGE *(on phone)*. ...now tell me about it.

AUNT TILLY *(interrupting)*. ...George, that woman's here again.

GEORGE. What woman?

AUNT TILLY *(nervously)*. Bank...bank examiner.

GEORGE. Oh...*(On phone.)* Talk to Aunt Tilly again a minute, will you? I'll be right back.

(GEORGE gives the phone to AUNT TILLY, puts down his wreath. VIOLET enters.)

GEORGE. Oh, hello, Vi.

VIOLET *(looking concerned and agitated)*. George, can I see you for a second?

GEORGE. Why, of course you can. Just step into my office. I'll be right there. *(GEORGE opens the door to his private office. VIOLET enters it. He shuts the door and crosses to MISS CARTER and shakes her hand.)* Good morning, Miss...

MISS CARTER. Carter—bank examiner.

GEORGE. Miss Carter, Merry Christmas.

MISS CARTER. Merry Christmas.

GEORGE. We're all excited around here. *(Shows her paper.)* My brother just got the Congressional Medal of Honor. The President just decorated him.

MISS CARTER. Well, I guess they do those things. I trust you had a good year.

GEORGE. Good year? Well, between you and me, Miss Carter, we're broke.

MISS CARTER. Very funny.

GEORGE. Well...*(Leading her into office.)*...now, come right in here, Miss Carter.

MISS CARTER *(as they go)*. Although I shouldn't wonder when you okay reverse charges on personal long distance calls.

AUNT TILLY. George, shall I hang up?

GEORGE. No, no. He wants to talk to Uncle Billy. You just hold on.

MISS CARTER *(in doorway)*. Now, if you'll cooperate, I'd like to finish with you by tonight. I want to spend Christmas in Elmira with my sister and her family.

GEORGE. I don't blame you at all, Miss Carter. Just step right in here. Uncle Billy has everything all laid out for you.

(MISS CARTER enters the office. GEORGE crosses to his office door and enters. UNCLE BILLY comes hurrying in.)

AUNT TILLY. Hurry, Uncle Billy, hurry. Long distance, Washington.

UNCLE BILLY. Not now. I can't talk to anyone now.

AUNT TILLY. But it's Harry, your nephew, remember? *(On phone.)* Here's your Uncle Billy, Harry. *(UNCLE BILLY picks up the phone and speaks distractedly without knowing what he is saying.)*

UNCLE BILLY *(on phone).* Hello...hello...Yes, Harry. Yes...everything...everything's fine.

(He hangs up agitatedly, muttering to himself. MISS CARTER sticks her head out of the office door.)

MISS CARTER. Mr. Bailey?

UNCLE BILLY. What? Oh, yes.

MISS CARTER. Oh, another Mr. Bailey. Well, you'll do just fine. Possibly better. May I see you in here for a moment, please? I have some questions.

UNCLE BILLY. Me? *(To himself.)* Oh, dear, dear. *(To MISS CARTER.)* Why, certain, yes, of course. I'll be right there. *(To AUNT TILLY.)* Where's George?

AUNT TILLY. In his office with Violet Peterson.

UNCLE BILLY. Oh, dear. Oh, dear, oh, dear. I need to see him as soon as he gets out. *(He slowly crosses and enters his office, closing the door after him.)*

(VIOLET and GEORGE enter from GEORGE's office. She is reading a letter GEORGE has just written for her.)

VIOLET. Character? If I had any character, I'd...

GEORGE. It takes a lot of character to leave your hometown and start all over again. *(He pulls some money from his pocket, and offers it to her.)*

VIOLET. No, George, don't...

GEORGE. Here, now, you're broke, aren't you?

VIOLET. I know, but...

GEORGE. What do you want to do, hock your furs, and that hat? Want to walk to New York? You know, they charge for meals and rent up there just the same as they do in Bedford Falls.

VIOLET *(taking money)*. Yeah—sure...

GEORGE. It's a loan. That's my business. Building and Loan. Besides, you'll get a job. Good luck to you. *(She looks at him and then says a strange thing.)*

VIOLET. I'm glad I know you, George Bailey. *(She reaches up and kisses him on the cheek, leaving lipstick.)*

GEORGE. Say hello to New York for me.

VIOLET. Yeah—yeah...sure I will.

GEORGE. And let's hear from you. *(VIOLET sees the lipstick on GEORGE's cheek, and dabs at it with her handkerchief.)* What's the matter? Merry Christmas, Vi.

VIOLET. Merry Christmas, George. *(She exits.)*

(MISS CARTER and UNCLE BILLY enter from the other office.)

MISS CARTER. Mr. Bailey, there seems to be a problem here.

GEORGE. A problem? How do you mean.

UNCLE BILLY. George, can I see you for a moment, alone. *(He grabs GEORGE and crosses downstage with him into a pool of light. Lights fade down and out on the Building and Loan wagon.)*

GEORGE. Uncle Billy, what is it?

UNCLE BILLY. Oh, George. *(He whispers in his ear.)*

GEORGE *(not wanting to believe what he heard)*. What?

UNCLE BILLY. Oh, dear, is that your bad ear?

GEORGE. No.

UNCLE BILLY. Then you did hear me.

GEORGE. I'm afraid so. How much? *(Again, UNCLE BILLY whispers in GEORGE's ear.)* That much? Are you sure? *(UNCLE BILLY nods his head.)* Now look, did you buy anything?

UNCLE BILLY. Nothing. Not even a stick of gum.

GEORGE. Are you sure you had the money with you?

UNCLE BILLY. Yes. I was counting it…I think.

GEORGE. You think? Uncle Billy, we've got to find that money!

UNCLE BILLY *(piteously)*. I'm no good to you, George. I…

GEORGE. Listen to me. Do you have any secret hiding places in your house? Someplace you could have put it? Someplace to hide the money?

UNCLE BILLY. No, nothing like that!

GEORGE. Listen to me! Listen to me! Think! Think!

UNCLE BILLY. I have been thinking, George. I have. And I can't think anymore. It hurts.

GEORGE. Now, listen to me. Where's that money, you stupid, silly old fool? Where's the money? Do you realize what this means? It means bankruptcy and scandal, and prison.

UNCLE BILLY. No, no, no.

GEORGE. Yes, that's what it means. One of us is going to jail! Well, it's not going to be me!

(GEORGE storms away. Lights cross fade: down and out on UNCLE BILLY; up on the Bailey sitting room. JANIE,

*age 9, can be heard practicing "Hark, the Herald Angels
Sing" on the piano in the next room. PETE, age 10, and
TOMMY, age 8, are adding the finishing touches to the
Christmas tree which stands in the corner near the fireplace. At a table, MARY is busy putting cellophane bows
and decorations on gift packages. GEORGE walks into the
area. Note: If technically you need more time at this point
to move on the Bailey's sitting room, you can have CAR-
OLERS cross the stage singing. GEORGE can pass them
and not acknowledge their pleasant greeting. When the setting is in place, GEORGE enters the scene.)*

MARY. Hello, darling.

CHILDREN. Hello, Daddy, hello, Daddy.

MARY *(indicating tree)*. How do you like it? *(GEORGE
sneezes violently.)*

MARY and CHILDREN. Bless you!

MARY. Did you bring the wreath?

PETE. Daddy, did you bring the Christmas wreath?

GEORGE. Wreath? What wreath?

MARY. The Christmas wreath for the window.

GEORGE *(gruffly)*. No. I left it at the office.

MARY. Is it snowing?

GEORGE. Yeah, just started.

MARY. Where's your coat and hat?

GEORGE. Left them at the office.

MARY *(concerned)*. What's the matter?

GEORGE *(bitterly)*. Nothing's the matter. Everything's all
right.

MARY. Isn't it wonderful about Harry? We're famous,
George. I'll bet I had fifty calls today about the parade, the
banquet. Your mother's so excited, she...

GEORGE *(interrupting sharply, referring to JANIE's piano playing).* Must she keep playing that?

TOMMY. She's practicing for the party tonight, Daddy.

PETE. Mommy says we can stay up 'til midnight and sing Christmas carols.

TOMMY. You can stay up too, Daddy.

PETE. Daddy, the Browns next door have a new car. You should see it.

GEORGE *(turns on him).* Well, what's the matter with our car? Isn't it good enough for you?

PETE. Yes, Daddy.

MARY *(to GEORGE).* Better hurry and shave, George. The families will be here soon.

GEORGE. Families! I don't want the families over here!

(At this moment, ZUZU enters, dressed in her nightgown.)

GEORGE. Zuzu! What's the matter with you?

MARY. Oh, she's got a cold. Caught it coming home from school. They gave her a flower for a prize and she didn't want to crush it so she didn't button up her coat. Go to bed, darling.

ZUZU. I want to get my flower a drink.

GEORGE. What do you have, Zuzu, a sore throat, or what?

MARY. Just a cold. The doctor says it's nothing serious.

GEORGE. The doctor? Was the doctor here?

MARY. Yes, I called him right away. He says it's nothing to worry about.

GEORGE *(to ZUZU as he picks her up).* Well, are you running a temperature, little one?

ZUZU. I don't think so.

MARY. Just a teensie one—ninety-nine, six. She'll be all right.

GEORGE (*putting ZUZU down*). Better get back upstairs, Zuzu. This floor is cold.

ZUZU. My flower...she needs a drink.

GEORGE (*sharply*). Now!

MARY (*gently, to make up for GEORGE's sharpness*). I'll bring a vase with water up in a minute. Now go along. (*ZUZU starts upstairs.*)

GEORGE. It's this old house. I don't know why we don't all have pneumonia. This drafty old barn! Might as well be living in a refrigerator! Why did we have to live here in the first place and stay around this measly, crummy old town?

MARY. George, what's wrong?

PETE. How do you spell frankincense?

GEORGE (*shouts*). I don't know. Ask your mother. (*The phone rings.*)

CHILDREN. Telephone.

MARY. I'll get it. (*On phone.*) Hello. Yes, this is Mrs. Bailey. Oh, thank you, Mrs. Welch. I'm sure she'll be all right. The doctor says that she ought to be out of bed in time to have her Christmas dinner.

GEORGE. Is that Zuzu's teacher?

MARY (*hand over mouthpiece*). Yes.

GEORGE. Let me speak to her. (*He snatches the phone from MARY.*) Hello. Hello, Mrs. Welch? This is George Bailey. I'm Zuzu's father. Say, what kind of a teacher are you, anyway? What do you mean sending her home like that, half naked? Do you realize she'll probably end up with pneumonia on account of you?

MARY (*shocked*). George! (*She puts a restraining hand on his arm. He shakes it off. She cannot know that GEORGE's tirade against Mrs. Welch is really a tirade against the world, against life itself, against God. Over the phone we hear Mrs. Welch's voice sputtering with protest.*)

GEORGE. Is this the sort of thing we pay taxes for—to have teachers like you? Silly, stupid, careless people who send our kids home without any clothes on? You know, maybe my kids aren't the best dressed kids, maybe they don't have any decent clothes...(*MARY succeeds in wresting the phone form GEORGE's hand.*) Aw, that stupid...(*MARY speaks quickly into phone.*)

MARY. Hello, Mrs. Welch. I want to apologize...hello... hello...(*To GEORGE.*) She's hung up.

GEORGE (*savagely*). I'll hang her up! (*The phone rings again.*) I'll get it. (*Answers phone.*) Hello? Who is this? Oh, Mr. Welch! I'm so glad you called. Gives me a chance to tell you what I really think of your wife. (*MARY once more tries to take the phone from him.*)

MARY. George...

GEORGE. What? Oh, you will, huh? Okay, Mr. Welch, any time you think you're man enough...Hello? He hung up. (*He hangs up the receiver.*)

PETE. Daddy, how do you spell "Hallelujah"?

GEORGE (*shouts*). How should I know? What do you think I am, a dictionary? (*Calling off stage to JANIE who has never stopped playing the piano.*) Janie, haven't you learned that silly tune, yet? You've played it over and over again. Now stop it! Stop it!

(*GEORGE runs out of the house area. Lights fade on MARY and the CHILDREN all huddled together. The two BOYS are crying and MARY is looking after GEORGE, quite worried. GEORGE crosses DL to MR. POTTER who is wheeled in by his GOON.*)

GEORGE. I'm in trouble, Mr. Potter. I need help. Through some sort of an accident my company's short in their accounts. The bank examiner's up there today. I've got to raise eight thousand dollars immediately.

POTTER *(casually)*. Oh, so that's what the reporters wanted to talk to you about?

GEORGE *(incredulous)*. The reporters?

POTTER. Yes. They called me up from your Building and Loan. Oh, there's a man over there from the D.A.'s office, too. He's looking for you.

GEORGE *(desperate)*. Please help me, Mr. Potter. Help me, won't you, please? Can't you see what it means to my family? I'll pay you any sort of a bonus on the loan...any interest. If you still want the Building and Loan, why I...

POTTER *(interrupting)*. George, could it possibly be there's a slight discrepancy in the books?

GEORGE. No, sir. There's nothing wrong with the books. I've just misplaced eight thousand dollars. I can't find it anywhere.

POTTER *(looking up)*. *You* misplaced eight thousand dollars?

GEORGE. Yes, sir.

POTTER. Have you notified the police?

GEORGE. No, sir. I didn't want the publicity. Harry's homecoming tomorrow...

POTTER *(snorts)*. They're going to believe that one. What've you been doing, George? Playing the market with the company's money?

GEORGE. No, sir. No, sir. I haven't.

POTTER. What is it—a woman then? You know, it's all over town that you've been giving money to Violet Peterson.

GEORGE *(incredulous)*. What?

POTTER. Not that it makes any difference to me, but why did you come to me? Why don't you go to Sam Wainwright and ask him for the money?

GEORGE. I can't get hold of him. He's in Europe.

POTTER. Well, what about all your other friends?

GEORGE. They don't have that kind of money, Mr. Potter. You know that. You're the only one in town that can help me.

POTTER. I see. I've suddenly become quite important. What kind of security would I have, George? Have you any stocks?

GEORGE *(shaking his head)*. No, sir.

POTTER. Bonds? Real estate? Collateral of any kind?

GEORGE *(pulls out policy)*. I have some life insurance, a fifteen thousand dollar policy.

POTTER. Yes...how much is your equity in it?

GEORGE. Five hundred dollars.

POTTER *(sarcastically)*. Look at you. You used to be so cocky! You were going to go out and conquer the world! You once called me a warped, frustrated old man. What are you but a warped, frustrated young man. A miserable little clerk crawling in here on your hands and knees and begging for help. No securities—no stocks— no bonds— nothing but a miserable little five hundred dollar equity in a life insurance policy. You're worth more dead than alive. Why don't you go to the riff-raff you love so much and ask them to let you have eight thousand dollars? You know why? Because they'd run you out of town on a rail...But I'll tell you what I'm going to do for you, George. Since the state examiner is still here, as a stockholder of Building and Loan, I'm going to swear out a warrant for your arrest. Misappropriation of funds—manipulation—malfeasance... *(GEORGE starts backing away.)*

GEORGE *(incredulously)*. No! No! No!

POTTER. All right, George, go ahead. You can't hide in a little town like this. *(His GOON turns and wheels POTTER out, stage R. GEORGE stands C stage not knowing which way to turn.)*

GEORGE. Oh, God, you've got to help me out here.

(He is joined by a group of TOWNSPEOPLE, entering stage R, singing "God Rest Ye Merry, Gentlemen." MR. and MRS. MARTINI, ERNIE and MR. WELCH are among them.)

MARTINI. George? George Bailey, is that you? Come on and join us.

GEORGE. Not tonight, Mr. Martini.

WELCH *(stepping out from the gathering).* Wait a minute? Did he call you George Bailey?

MARTINI. That's right. This is Mr. George Bailey, brother of the young man who has just been given the Congressional Medal of Honor. *(Without any warning, the burly man throws a vicious punch at GEORGE who goes down hard. The singing stops and all the TOWNSPEOPLE gather around.)*

WELCH. And the next time you talk to my wife like that you'll get worse. She cried for an hour and wouldn't even come out with us tonight.

ERNIE. That's enough, Mr. Welch, that's enough.

WELCH. It isn't enough she slaves teaching your stupid kids how to read and write, you have to bawl her out...

MARTINI. Mr. Welch!

WELCH. Aw, to hell with it. I'm going home. *(He exits, stage L.)*

MRS. MARTINI. Come on, everybody. This is Christmas Eve. We're supposed to be spreading good cheer.

ERNIE. Yes, aren't we going to sing anymore?

MARTINI. Of course we are. Come on, everybody. *(MAR-TINI starts singing again. Everyone else joins in. They all move away except ERNIE who stays with GEORGE and helps him up.)*

ERNIE. Are you all right, George?

GEORGE *(sarcastically)*. Sure.

ERNIE. You want me to take you home?

GEORGE. No! Please. I'll be fine. I'm waiting for someone. Go on with your friends.

ERNIE. You sure?

GEORGE *(to himself)*. Where's my insurance policy?

ERNIE. What?

GEORGE. Just leave me alone, Ernie. Please. Leave me alone.

(MARTINI enters.)

MARTINI. Ernie, are you coming?

ERNIE. I'll be right there. *(To GEORGE.)* You're sure you'll be all right, George?

GEORGE. I'm sure, Ernie. Thank you.

ERNIE. Well then...Merry Christmas. *(He follows MARTINI off.)*

GEORGE. Merry Christmas. *(GEORGE is left alone. He takes out his insurance policy, looks at it, breaks down, and falls to his knees. He raises his head to Heaven and desperately sends up a prayer.)* God...God...Dear Father in Heaven, I'm not a praying man, but if you're up there and you can hear me, show me the way. I'm at the end of my rope. Show me the way, God.

(CLARENCE appears as if out of nowhere.)

CLARENCE. And that's where I came in.

GEORGE. You mean, you actually heard my prayer up there?

CLARENCE. Yours and over a dozen others. You'd be surprised how many people are concerned about you.

GEORGE. Not after they find out that I've ruined their lives.

CLARENCE. You haven't ruined their lives, George. Besides, it wasn't your fault.

GEORGE. I'm the president of the company. I'm the one to be held accountable. Ask Mr. Potter. He'll tell you.

CLARENCE. And you think killing yourself would make everyone feel happier?

GEORGE. Oh, I don't know. I suppose it would have been better if I'd never been born at all.

CLARENCE. What'd you say?

GEORGE. I said I wish I'd never been born.

CLARENCE. Oh, you mustn't say things like that. You... *(Gets an idea.)*...wait a minute. Wait a minute. That's an idea. *(Glances up toward Heaven.)* What do you think? Yeah, that'll do it. All right. *(To GEORGE.)* You've got your wish. You've never been born. *(As CLARENCE speaks this line, there is a strong wind and a bright light that comes up for a moment and then returns to normal. CLARENCE looks upward.)* You don't have to make all that fuss about it. *(As CLARENCE speaks, GEORGE cocks his head curiously, favoring his deaf ear, more interested in his hearing than in what CLARENCE has said.)*

GEORGE. What did you say?

CLARENCE. You've never been born. You don't exist. You haven't a care in the world. *(GEORGE feels his ear as CLARENCE talks.)* No worries—no obligations—no eight thousand dollars to get—no Potter looking for you with the sheriff.

GEORGE. Say something else in that ear.

CLARENCE *(bending down)*. Sure. You can hear out of it.

GEORGE. Well, that's the doggonedest thing...I haven't heard anything out of that ear since I was a kid. What's going on here?

(The MEN from townspeople grouping enter. They are singing again but it's obvious that this time they are not caroling—they're drunk. MARTINI and WELCH are two of the singers. Both are carrying bottles.)

MARTINI. Hey, look over there. There're two more suckers. Let's sing to them. *(The MEN all laugh and cross down to CLARENCE and GEORGE.)*

MEN *(singing off key)*. "We wish you a Merry Christmas. We wish you a Merry Christmas."

GEORGE. Dominic?

MARTINI. That's my name and this is my poison. Want some?

GEORGE. Mr. Martini, don't you recognize me?

WELCH. Dominic, he knows your name. Now we've got to sing.

GEORGE. Where's your wife? Where's Mrs. Martini?

MARTINI. Shhhh. She's home. They're all home. And that makes it a Merry Christmas, doesn't it, gents? *(He laughs loudly and the other MEN join in.)*

GEORGE. But I saw her just a minute ago...her and lots of women and children too.

WELCH. Where? What are you talking about? *(Threatening GEORGE, as if he was going to hit him again.)* You're not about to snitch on us, are you?

GEORGE. Wait a minute. I know you. You hit me just a minute ago.

WELCH. I did? Did you hear that? I already hit him. *(To GEORGE.)* Did it hurt? *(He laughs outrageously. The other MEN join him.)* Here, let me try again.

MARTINI *(stopping WELCH, as he had tried before)*. Aw, come on. Leave the sucker alone. He's worse off than we are.

(GOWER enters, also drunk, but unlike the others, a real panhandler.)

ERNIE *(seeing GOWER)*. Look out. Here comes that panhandler. He's caught up with us again.

MARTINI. Come on, let's get out of here.

WELCH *(still holding onto GEORGE)*. Aw, let me hit him first. *(To GEORGE.)* I promise, I'll remember it this time.

GOWER *(calling out as he lumbers down)*. Hey, one of ya got a dime or two you could spare? *(Seeing the bottles.)* Or a drink? I'll settle for a drink.

GEORGE *(pulling away from WELCH and crossing to GOWER)*. Mr. Gower! This is George Bailey! Don't you remember me?

MARTINI. I tell you, come on. I don't like messing around that guy.

GEORGE. You own the corner drugstore and I used to work for you when I was a kid. Don't you remember?

WELCH. Now I know I don't like you. That rumhead spent twenty years in jail for poisoning a kid.

MARTINI. That's right. And if you know him, you must be a jail-bird yourself. Come on, men, let's get out of here.

GOWER *(following them)*. Wait a minute. Wait for me.

CLARENCE. You see, George, you were not there to stop Gower from putting that poison into the...

GEORGE. What do you mean, I wasn't there? I remember distinctly...Look, who are you?

CLARENCE. I told you, George. I'm your guardian angel.

GEORGE. But I don't get it.

CLARENCE. It's what you asked for...what you wanted. Don't you understand? It's all because you were not born.

GEORGE. Not born?

CLARENCE. That's right.

GEORGE. But if I wasn't born, who am I?

CLARENCE. You're nobody. You have no identity.

GEORGE. What do you mean, no identity? My name's George Bailey. I was born July 12, 1907 right here in Bedford Falls.

CLARENCE. You won't find any public record of it. Besides, this isn't Bedford Falls anymore. It's Pottersville.

GEORGE. Pottersville? No! No!

CLARENCE. I'm afraid so. And there is no George Bailey. Never has been. You see, you've been given a great gift, George. Just what you asked for, a chance to see what the world would be like without you.

(CLARENCE turns and where he looks off, VIOLET walks into the scene. Her profession is obvious by the clothes she wears. CLARENCE fades out of the scene and exits.)

GEORGE. Violet?

VIOLET. That's what they call me.

GEORGE. Oh, am I glad to see you.

VIOLET *(flattered by the come on)*. Well, I'm glad to see you too. New in town? Who gave you my name?

GEORGE *(anxious and insistent)*. I'm George!

VIOLET. Of course you are. And if anyone asks me, I've never seen or even heard of you before.

GEORGE. But you have. I'm George Bailey. We grew up together.

VIOLET. I don't think so, good looking. But I sure wish we had.

GEORGE. Violet, you've got to remember.

VIOLET. Well, I've got all night. You want to tell me about it?

GEORGE. Your name is Violet Peterson. You were born in...in 1910, no, wait a minute, 1911. And you graduated, right here, from the local high school...

VIOLET. Wait a minute. What are you, some sort of private eye? I should have known. Don't you guys ever give it a rest? It's Christmas Eve, for God's sake.

GEORGE. No. You don't understand.

VIOLET. Oh, yes, I do. Well, "See no evil, hear no evil, speak no evil," that's my motto. So, give it a rest and get out of here.

GEORGE. Violet!

VIOLET. Or, I'll make a telephone call, George, or whatever your name is. And I don't think you'd want me to do that. Merry Christmas. *(She turns and walks off.)*

(Lights come up on a porch with a sign on the wall by the door reading "Ma Bailey's Boarding House.")

GEORGE. Boarding House. What's going on here?

(He walks tentatively up on the porch and rings the bell. The door opens and a woman appears. It is MRS. BAILEY, but she has changed amazingly. Her face is harsh and tired. In her eyes, once kindly and understanding, there is now cold suspicion. She gives no sign that she knows GEORGE.)

MA BAILEY. Well? *(She waits for a response but GEORGE doesn't answer. He can't believe what he sees.)* What do you want? If you're looking for a room there's no vacancy. *(She starts to close the door, but GEORGE stops her.)*

GEORGE. No, wait a minute. Please. I'm lost and I need to sort things out. Please let me in.

MA BAILEY. I told you I've got no vacancy. Besides, I don't take in strangers unless they're referred by someone. Try over on Maple Street. One sixty-three Maple. *(Again, she starts to shut the door.)*

GEORGE. I know your brother-in-law, Uncle Billy.

MA BAILEY *(suspiciously)*. How do you know him?

GEORGE. I've seen him around.

MA BAILEY. When? When did you see him around?

GEORGE. Today, over at his house.

MA BAILEY. That's a lie. He's been in the state asylum for over five years, ever since he lost his business.

GEORGE. Harry. Your son, Harry.

MA BAILEY *(really angry now)*. My only son broke through the ice and was drowned at the age of nine.

GEORGE. No! He's alive! He went to war and got the Congressional Medal of Honor! He's a hero, and he's coming home tomorrow.

MA BAILEY. I'm going to call the police.

(She slams the door. GEORGE turns, looking totally dumbfounded and disoriented. He crosses off the porch. CLARENCE walks into his light.)

CLARENCE. Strange, isn't it? Each man's life touches so many other lives, and when he isn't around he leaves an awful hole, doesn't he?

GEORGE *(still talking about HARRY)*. He saved the lives of every man on that transport. It was headlines in all the newspapers.

CLARENCE. Every man on that transport died. Harry wasn't there to save them because you weren't there to save Harry. You see, George, you really had a wonderful life. Don't you see what a mistake it would be to throw it away?

GEORGE. Clarence...

CLARENCE. Yes, George?

GEORGE. Where's Mary?

CLARENCE. Oh, well, I don't think...

GEORGE. If you know where she is, tell me.

CLARENCE. You're not going to like it, George. *(GEORGE grabs CLARENCE by the coat collar and shakes him.)*

GEORGE. Tell me where she is. Is she alive?

CLARENCE. Yes, she's alive...and she never married. But she's not the Mary you know. Something happened...

(MARY enters, carrying a book. She is very different—no buoyancy in her walk, none of MARY's abandon and love of life. Glasses, no make-up, lips compressed, elbows close to her body. She looks dried up and tired. GEORGE sees her over CLARENCE's shoulder.)

GEORGE. Mary? *(He moves slowly toward her.)*

CLARENCE *(to himself, as he fades out of the scene and exits)*. There must be some easier way for me to get my wings. *(MARY is looking down and does not see GEORGE, who is standing in her path, until she is nearly up to him.)*

GEORGE. Mary.

MARY *(looking up at him, scared to death)*. Who are you? What do you want?

GEORGE. It's me, George. Don't you know me?

MARY. Get away from me. I'll scream.

GEORGE. Mary, what happened to us?

MARY. I don't know what you're talking about.

GEORGE. Mary, look at me. I'm George. I'm your husband, George.

MARY. No! No, leave me alone. Don't touch me! *(She calls out.)* Somebody, help! *(To GEORGE.)* Please! I can't stand anyone to touch me! I'll scream. *(She turns and runs off.)* Help! Somebody, please! Help!

GEORGE *(calling after her).* Mary! Mary! *(He runs until he realizes that he is back on the bridge. He stops and looks out.)* Clarence! Clarence! Help me, Clarence. Get me back. Get me back. I don't care what happens to me. Only get me back to my wife and my kids. Help me, Clarence, please. Please! I want to live again!

(As before, the light on GEORGE gets very bright, there's a strange sound as the wind builds and then, all returns to normal. BERT, the policeman, comes running in.)

BERT. Hey, George! George! You all right? *(GEORGE backs away.)* Hey, what's the matter?

GEORGE. I didn't do anything to her, honest.

BERT. What are you talking about? What in the Sam Hill are you yelling for, George?

GEORGE. Don't...George? Bert, do you know me?

BERT. Know you? Are you kiddin'? I've been looking all over town trying to find you. Half the town's out looking for you.

GEORGE. Mary! Mary!

BERT. Yeah, Mary called. And so did Martini, and your Uncle Billy, and even your mother called. So, what's going on George?

GEORGE. What's going on? Why, look around you, Bert. It's breathing, it's moving, it's alive. Oh, Merry Christmas, Bert. *(He throws his arms around BERT and gives him a big hug.)*

BERT. I think I better take you home.

GEORGE. No, Bert, I'm fine, honestly, I'm fine.

(Lights come up on the Bailey's home and fade on BERT. GEORGE walks into the area. Waiting for him is MISS CARTER.)

GEORGE *(excitedly).* Mary...Well, hello, Miss Bank Examiner!

MISS CARTER. Mr. Bailey, you have a deficit we must talk about.

GEORGE. Yes. Isn't it wonderful? Merry Christmas! *(He kisses her on the forehead.)* Where's Mary? *(Calling.)* Mary! Oh, look at this wonderful drafty house! Mary! Mary! *(To MISS CARTER.)* Have you seen my wife?

(GEORGE's CHILDREN come running into the room.)

CHILDREN. Merry Christmas, Daddy!

GEORGE. Oh, you wonderful kids! I could eat you up! *(They all hug each other.)* But where's your mother?

JANIE. She went looking for you with Uncle Billy.

(At this moment, MARY enters the scene.)

MARY. George! Darling! *(Seeing MISS CARTER.)* Oh, hello.

GEORGE. Hallelujah!

MARY. George, darling! Where have you been? *(GEORGE and MARY embrace tearfully.)* Oh, George, George, George.

GEORGE. Mary! Let me touch you! Oh, you're real!

MARY. Oh, George, George!

GEORGE. You have no idea what happened to me.

MARY. You have no idea what happened...*(He stops her with a kiss.)* Come on now. You stand right over here, by the tree. Right here and don't move. They're coming now, George. I hear them. It's a miracle! A miracle.

(Ad lib sounds of excited crowd can be heard. UNCLE BILLY, face flushed, carrying a clothes basket filled with money, bursts in. He is followed by BERT and the rest of the TOWNSPEOPLE.)

MARY. Come in, Uncle Billy, Bert. Everybody! In here. *(UNCLE BILLY dumps the basketful of money out onto the table that stands by the tree. The money overflows and falls all over.)*

UNCLE BILLY. Isn't it wonderful? Mary did it, George! She told a few people you were in trouble and they scattered all over town collecting money. They didn't ask any questions—just said: "If George is in trouble—count on me." You never saw anything like it. *(Each individual comes up with his or her gift.)*

ERNIE. What is this, George? Another run on the bank? *(ERNIE adds his money to the pile.)*

MARTINI. I wouldn't have a roof over my head if it wasn't for you, George. Merry Christmas.

MISS ANDREWS. Glad to do it, George.

MRS. THOMPSON. Anytime for you, Mr. Bailey.

GOWER (*looking prosperous and clean shaven again*). I made the rounds of all my charge accounts, George.

(*VIOLET arrives, and takes out the money GEORGE had given her for her trip to New York.*)

VIOLET. I'm not going to go, George. I changed my mind.

ERNIE. Just a minute. Quiet, everybody. Quiet—quiet. Now, this is from London. (*Reading a telegram.*) "Mr. Gower cables you need cash. Stop. My office instructed to advance you up to twenty-five thousand dollars. Stop. Merry Christmas, Sam Wainwright." (*The CROWD breaks into a cheer as ERNIE drops the telegram on top of the pile of money on the table. Someone starts singing "Hark the Herald Angels Sing," and the entire CROWD joins in the singing.*)

(*HARRY, in Naval uniform, and carrying CLARENCE's copy of* Tom Sawyer, *enters and rushes into the space.*)

HARRY. George!

GEORGE. Harry! Harry!

HARRY. Well, it looks like I got here just in time. Anyone got any wine...champagne? I want to make a toast. To my big brother, George. The richest man in town! (*Once more the CROWD breaks into cheering and applause. HARRY silences them.*) Wait a minute. Wait a minute. I forgot. Some crazy little ol' man handed me this at the airport. Made me promise I would hand it to you personally. (*Hands GEORGE the book he has been holding.*)

MARY *(reading from the cover)*. Tom Sawyer? Who would give you a beat-up copy of *Tom Sawyer? (GEORGE opens the cover and reads the inscription.)*

GEORGE. "Dear George, remember no man is a failure who has friends. Thanks for the wings, Love, Clarence." *(GEORGE looks up. Everyone is looking at him quizzically.)* A Christmas present from a very dear friend of mine. Just like all of you. Merry Christmas, everybody.

ZUZU. Listen, Daddy.

GEORGE. What, darling?

ZUZU. Hear the bell? Teacher says, every time a bell rings an angel gets his wings.

GEORGE. That's right, that's right. *(He looks up toward the ceiling and winks.)* Attaboy, Clarence. *(Everyone starts singing* "Auld Lang Syne." *MISS CARTER crosses to GEORGE and while he watches, she tears up the balance sheet she has brought with her and drops it on the table with all the money. GEORGE kisses MARY then looks up and winks as if to say, "Attaboy, Clarence." The voices of all singing swell into a final crescendo as the curtain falls.)*

THE END

DIRECTOR'S NOTES

DIRECTOR'S NOTES

DIRECTOR'S NOTES